Monkeys
and other Primates

Rebecca Sjonger & Bobbie Kalman

🌲 Crabtree Publishing Company

www.crabtreebooks.com

Monkeys
and other Primates

Created by Bobbie Kalman

Dedicated by Heather Fitzpatrick
To my daughter Emma Fitzpatrick Nesbitt—my cute little monkey

Editor-in-Chief
Bobbie Kalman

Writing team
Rebecca Sjonger
Bobbie Kalman

Substantive editor
Kelley MacAulay

Project editor
Reagan Miller

Editors
Molly Aloian
Robin Johnson
Kathryn Smithyman

Design
Katherine Kantor

Production coordinator
Heather Fitzpatrick

Photo research
Crystal Foxton

Consultant
Patricia Loesche, Ph.D., Animal Behavior Program,
Department of Psychology, University of Washington

Illustrations
Barbara Bedell: pages 5 (bonobo, bushbaby, and gorilla), 7 (bottom), 30 (top left and
    bottom left and right), 32 (gorillas)
Katherine Kantor: pages 5 (chimpanzee), 30 (top right), 32 (chimpanzees)
Vanessa Parson-Robbs: pages 5 (loris), 32 (lorises)
Bonna Rouse: pages 5 (tarsier), 6, 7 (top), 30 (bottom middle), 32 (backbones, lungs,
    and tarsiers)

Photographs
Toni Angermayer/Photo Researchers, Inc.: page 24
Big Stock Photo: Sergey Pristyazhnyuk: page 4 (top right)
Bruce Coleman Inc.: Rod Williams: page 11 (left)
© Haring, David/Animals Animals - Earth Scenes: page 28
iStockphoto.com: Tom De Bruyne: page 4 (bottom left); Holger Ehlers: page 25 (right);
    Jeff Gynane: page 15 (right); Michael Lynch: page 25 (left); Kevin Tate: page 27 (left)
Steve Knott/Alamy: page 23 (top)
Tim Miller: page 4 (top left)
Minden Pictures: Frans Lanting: page 22
© NHPA/Daniel Heuclin: page 14 (left)
© Anup Shah/naturepl.com: page 19
Other images by Corbis, Corel, Creatas, Digital Stock, Digital Vision, and Photodisc

Crabtree Publishing Company

www.crabtreebooks.com   1-800-387-7650

Cataloging-in-Publication Data
Sjonger, Rebecca.
    Monkeys and other primates / Rebecca Sjonger & Bobbie Kalman.
      p. cm. -- (What kind of animal is it?)
    Includes index.
    ISBN-13: 978-0-7787-2165-9 (rlb)
    ISBN-10: 0-7787-2165-5 (rlb)
    ISBN-13: 978-0-7787-2223-6 (pbk)
    ISBN-10: 0-7787-2223-6 (pbk)
    1. Primates--Juvenile literature. 2. Monkeys--Juvenile literature. I. Kalman, Bobbie.
II. Title. III. Series.
    QL737.P9S53 2005
    599.8--dc22
                                                                2005023001
                                                                        LC

**Published in
the United States**

PMB16A
350 Fifth Ave.
Suite 3308
New York, NY
10118

**Published
in Canada**

616 Welland Ave.,
St. Catharines, Ontario
Canada
L2M 5V6

**Published in the
United Kingdom**

73 Lime Walk
Headington
Oxford
OX3 7AD
United Kingdom

**Published
in Australia**

386 Mt. Alexander Rd.,
Ascot Vale (Melbourne)
VIC 3032

Contents

All kinds of primates!

Primates are animals. There are many **species**, or kinds of primates. Each primate belongs to a group. There are four groups of primates. The four groups are shown on these pages.

1. The largest group of primates is called Old World monkeys.

marmosets

2. Another group of primates is called New World monkeys. Marmosets, tamarins, and New World monkeys make up this group.

tamarin

New World monkey

4

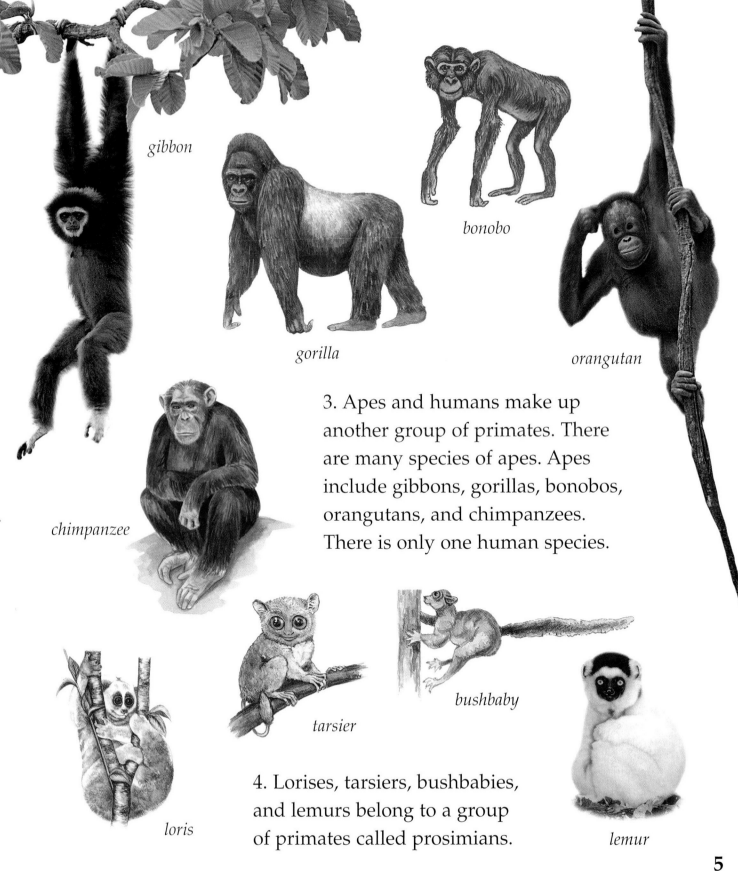

gibbon

bonobo

gorilla

orangutan

chimpanzee

3. Apes and humans make up another group of primates. There are many species of apes. Apes include gibbons, gorillas, bonobos, orangutans, and chimpanzees. There is only one human species.

tarsier

bushbaby

loris

4. Lorises, tarsiers, bushbabies, and lemurs belong to a group of primates called prosimians.

lemur

5

Primates are mammals

Primates are **mammals**. All mammals have **backbones** inside their bodies. A backbone is a group of bones in the middle of an animal's back.

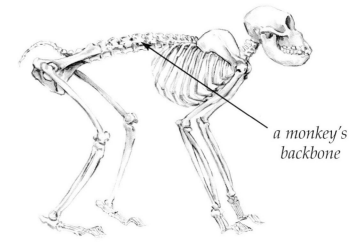

a monkey's backbone

These Old World monkeys have backbones.

6

Breathing air

Mammals breathe air to stay alive. Like all mammals, primates breathe air using **lungs**. Lungs are body parts that take in air. Lungs also let out air.

a gorilla's lungs

More about mammals

Mammals are animals that
- **nurse** when they are babies (See page 21.)
- are **warm-blooded** (See page 8.)
- have fur or hair on their bodies (See page 9.)

Warm blood

Like all mammals, primates are **warm-blooded** animals. The bodies of warm-blooded animals always stay about the same temperature, in both hot weather and cold weather.

These snow monkeys live in Japan. Japan is warm in summer, but cold in winter. A snow monkey's body temperature is the same in summer as it is in winter.

Fur or hair

All primates have fur or hair on their bodies. Most primates have fur. Their fur helps keep them warm and dry.

People have hair on their bodies.
The girl, shown right, has long hair.

Different primates have fur of different colors. These lemurs have black-and-white fur.
Their fur is silky.

9

Primate bodies

All primates have arms, legs, hands, and feet. Primates also have fingers and toes. Most primates have thumbs. They use their fingers, toes, and thumbs to hold objects. All primates have nails on their fingers and toes. Having nails helps primates pick up small objects. Some primates have tails. A few primates can hold objects using their tails.

This orangutan grabs onto vines using its fingers and toes.

Big or small?

The bodies of different primates are different sizes. Some primates have large bodies. Gorillas are the largest primates. Other primates have small bodies. Mouse lemurs are some of the smallest primates.

A mouse lemur's body is about the same size as a mouse's body.

Male gorillas, such as the one shown above, are the largest primates.

Primate homes

Different primates live in different parts of the world. Most primates live in places where the weather is always warm. Other primates live in places that are warm in summer and cold in winter.

Many primates live in Africa and South America. These places are always warm. The baboons in the picture above live in Africa. Baboons are Old World monkeys.

In the trees

Most primates live in forest **habitats**. A habitat is the natural place where an animal lives. Many primates are good climbers! They spend a lot of time in trees. Primates climb trees using their strong arms, hands, legs, and feet. Other primates use their strong legs to leap from tree to tree.

Primates with small bodies spend more time in trees than they do on the ground. This New World monkey lives mainly in trees.

Primates with large bodies spend most of their time on the ground. Chimpanzees usually stay on the ground.

Food and water

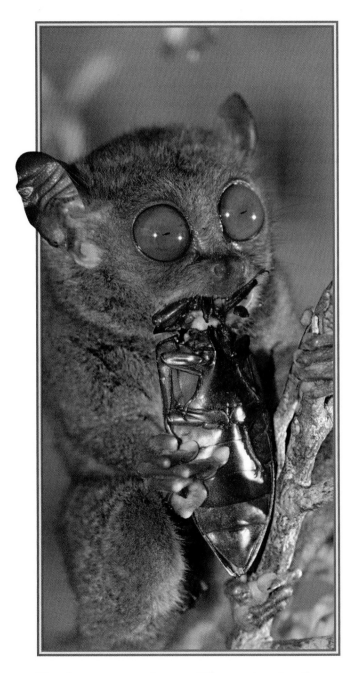

Different primates eat different foods. Some primates are **herbivores**. Herbivores are animals that eat mainly plants. A few primates are **carnivores**. Carnivores are animals that eat other animals. Most primates are **omnivores**. Omnivores are animals that eat both plants and other animals.

Tarsiers are carnivores. They eat animals such as lizards, birds, and insects. This tarsier is eating an insect.

Large primates often look for food during the day. Chimpanzees are large primates. They look for food during the day. Small primates look for food at night.

Crowned lemurs are herbivores.
They eat mainly fruit.

Thirsty primates

Primates need to drink water to stay alive. They often drink from puddles. They scoop up water using their hands. The gorilla above is using its hands to scoop up water from a river. Some primates use leaves to collect water. They soak the leaves in water and then squeeze the water into their mouths.

Groups called troups

Most kinds of primates live in groups. These groups are called **troups**. Some primate troups are large. Large troups may have over 20 primates! Other primate troups are small. Small troups may have only two primates.

Large troups are made up of many males, females, and young primates. Mountain gorillas live in large troups.

Part of a family

A primate troup is like a family. The older primates in the troup take care of the younger primates. Young primates, such as this baby monkey, learn by watching older primates. They learn how to find food, collect water, and climb trees.

Sending messages

Primates send messages to one another in different ways. They often use sounds and actions to send messages. Some primates hoot or grunt to greet one another. Primates may also stomp their feet or hold out their hands when they are begging for food.

This Old World monkey is showing its sharp teeth. It seems to be angry or excited. Monkeys also roar loudly to warn other animals to stay away!

Chimpanzees often kiss and hug each other to make up after a fight!

Musical messages

Gibbons send messages by making loud high-pitched calls. These calls are known as **songs**. Gibbons may sing songs to warn other animals to stay away. Some gibbons sing for as long as fifteen minutes without stopping!

This gibbon mother is singing to keep other animals away from her baby.

Primate babies

Primate babies are born. Animals that are born are not inside eggs when they come out of the bodies of their mothers. Both mother and father primates care for their babies. Other members of the troup may also watch over the babies.

Most primate mothers give birth to one or two babies at a time.

Drinking milk

Primate parents care for their babies for at least one year. The babies drink milk from the bodies of their mothers. Drinking mother's milk is called nursing. The babies nurse many times a day. As they get older, the young primates stop nursing. They find their own food.

This baby chimpanzee is nursing.

Many monkeys!

There are more than 80 kinds of Old World monkeys! Old World monkeys live in Africa, Asia, and Europe. Most species of Old World monkeys live mainly in trees. Many have short tails. They cannot hold objects with their tails. Old World monkeys hold objects using their thumbs and their big toes.

Old World monkeys, such as this baboon, have pads of skin on their bottoms.

Primates with pouches

Many species of Old World monkeys have **pouches** inside their mouths. Pouches are small pockets. The monkeys fill their pouches with food. They carry the food back to their troups and share it with the other monkeys.

This Old World monkey is filling its pouches with grass and leaves.

A few species of Old World monkeys, such as macaques, live mainly on the ground. These macaques are eating grass and plants.

More monkey business

New World monkeys, marmosets, and tamarins live in Central America and South America. These primates live only in trees. They do not spend time on the ground. Most New World monkeys can hang from branches using their long tails. Most marmosets and tamarins cannot use their tails to hang from branches.

Marmosets and tamarins use their sharp claws to hold on to tree branches. The primates above are tamarins.

What is the difference?

New World monkeys do not look the same as Old World monkeys. The charts on this page show how these monkeys are different.

Old World monkeys

- Old World monkeys have nostrils that point downward.
- Old World monkeys can hold objects using their thumbs.
- Old World monkeys have pads on their bottoms.

New World monkeys

- New World monkeys have nostrils that point sideways.
- New World monkeys cannot hold objects using their thumbs.
- New World monkeys do not have pads on their bottoms.

All about apes

Bonobos, chimpanzees, gorillas, orangutans, and gibbons are all known as apes. Apes live mainly in Africa and Asia. You can tell if a primate is an ape by looking at its bottom! Unlike many other primates, apes do not have tails.

Many apes build nests using tree branches and leaves. This chimpanzee mother and baby are resting in a nest.

Harmless herbivores

Apes are the strongest primates. Most apes are herbivores. They eat a lot of food, such as fruits, leaves, and flowers. The mountain gorilla, shown below, is eating leaves.

Most apes spend time in trees and on the ground. Gibbons spend most of their time in trees. Their bodies are smaller than the bodies of most other apes. Gibbons are good climbers and swingers. They swing from branch to branch faster than other apes can.

Prosimians

Prosimians live in Africa and Asia. They live mainly in trees. Most prosimians look for food at night. They have large eyes that help them see in the dark. Lorises, such as the one on the left, move slowly through the trees. They eat caterpillars and other insects that move slowly, too.

This loris uses its large eyes to look for insects at night.

Ring-tailed lemurs are among the few prosimians that spend time on the ground. Other prosimians stay high up in trees. These ring-tailed lemurs are resting on a fallen tree.

Where in the world?

Primates live in many parts of the world. Most primates live in South America, Africa, and Asia. Some primates live in Europe and Central America. Look at the map below and then answer the questions on page 31.

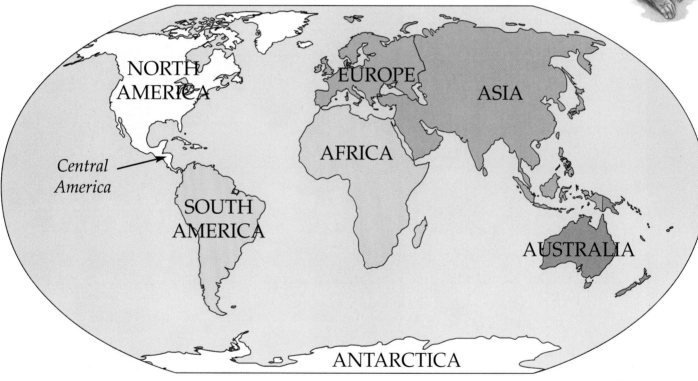

NORTH AMERICA

EUROPE

ASIA

Central America

AFRICA

SOUTH AMERICA

AUSTRALIA

ANTARCTICA

2. This bushbaby is a prosimian. On which continents do prosimians live? Turn to page 28 for a clue.

3. This chimpanzee is part of the ape group. Where does it live? Think hard! Turn to page 26 for help.

1. Old World monkeys live on three continents. Turn to page 22 to find out where they live.

4. Primates in the New World monkey group live in two parts of the world. See page 24 to find out where they live.

Answers

1. Africa, Asia, and Europe
2. Africa and Asia
3. Africa and Asia
4. South America and Central America

Words to know and Index

babies
pages 7, 17, 19, 20-21, 26
(**nursing** pages 7, 21)

backbones
page 6

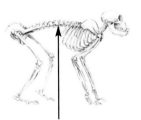

chimpanzees
pages 5, 13, 14,
18, 21, 26, 31

gibbons
pages 5, 19, 26, 27

gorillas
pages 5, 7, 11,
15, 16, 26, 27

lemurs
pages 5, 9,
11, 15, 29

lorises
pages 5, 28

lungs
page 7

Other index words

apes pages 5, 26-27, 31
bonobos pages 5, 26
bushbabies pages 5, 31
fur pages 7, 9
marmosets pages 4, 24
prosimians pages 5,
   28-29, 31
tamarins pages 4, 24
warm blood pages 7, 8

monkeys
pages 4, 6, 8,
   12, 13, 17, 18,
   22-25, 31

orangutans
pages 5, 10, 26

tarsiers
pages 5, 14

32